Legal Experiments: Mission Impossible?

Erasmus University Rotterdam

Legal Experiments: Mission Impossible?

Inaugural Lecture

Delivered on the occasion of accepting the position of holder of the Erasmus Chair of Internationalization at the Erasmus University Rotterdam on Thursday, 6 December 2012

Christoph Engel

eleven
international publishing

Published, sold and distributed by Eleven International Publishing
P.O. Box 85576
2508 CG The Hague
The Netherlands
Tel.: +31 70 33 070 33
Fax: +31 70 33 070 30
e-mail: sales@budh.nl
www.elevenpub.com

Sold and distributed in USA and Canada
International Specialized Book Services
920 NE 58th Avenue, Suite 300
Portland, OR 97213-3786, USA
Tel: 1-800-944-6190 (toll-free)
Fax: +1 503 280-8832
orders@isbs.com
www.isbs.com

Eleven International Publishing is an imprint of Boom uitgevers Den Haag.

ISBN 978-94-6212-002-0

Printed in The Netherlands

Table of Contents

Rector Magnificus, esteemed colleagues, dear friends,

1 Introduction

Beware of zealots! The good news is: they are likely to move the world. The bad news is: they are likely to move the world. For most legal scholars, this glass is rather half empty. They are suspicious if one of their colleagues seems too engaged with a perspective, an approach, a method. To lawyers, what other disciplines would welcome as enthusiasm, devotion and specialization smells like narrow-mindedness, bias and intellectual poverty. Such reticence is most pronounced if a lawyer openly adopts a methodology from the social sciences. Isn't the discipline rightly called 'jurisprudence', not 'jurisscience'? Legal scholarship, of course, but legal science? Isn't that an oxymoron? Sceptics frown even more if this scientific methodology seems to be a direct import from the natural sciences. A legal lab? Are paragraphs now to be treated as molecules? If the economists desire to publish in *Science* and *Nature*, let them do so. Lawyers should resist the next scientific fad and remain firmly grounded in the law as it stands and in the problems of life it is meant to govern!

And yet experiments on legal issues are not as outlandish as it may seem. There is an old tradition of lawyers collaborating with psychologists, with two well-regarded specialized journals, *Psychology, Public Policy & the Law*, and *Law and Human Behaviour*. This line of research has been particularly interested in police investigations and in interaction in the courtroom. It has for instance tried to understand the conditions for line-ups leading to false recognition, or it has tested mock jurors on the dynamics of finding consensus. The typical method in law and psychology is a vignette study. Participants see a series of hypotheticals and are asked how they judge them or how they would act, were they in that situation. Experiments are also a tried-and-tested tool in criminology, again with a specialized journal, the *Journal of Experimental Criminology*. Criminologists have mainly run field experiments, manipulating police strategies or the sanctions meted out to convicts.

The only true novelty is the advent of what is best called experimental law and economics. This recent line of research applies the methodology of experimental economics to legal issues. It differs from the methodologies prevalent in psychology and criminology in a number of respects. The typical design is free from context. Participants are exposed to a naked incentive structure. Usually, experiments are interactive. The situation participants are faced with is real, not hypothetical. Real money is at stake. Usually, complete anonymity is guaranteed. Normally, the exclusive channel of communication between the participants is their actions, which are recorded on a computer network. Often, the experiment is repeated multiple times so that learning and interactive dynamics can be studied. Since these experiments test incentive structures, clear predictions may be derived from theory.

All of these features give the experimenter better control. The claim becomes credible that the one treatment manipulation has indeed caused an observed difference in behaviour. Yet the price experimenters pay for the increase in control is that these experiments are even more like science, and distance themselves even more from the traditional legal discourse. In this lecture, I try to take the concerns seriously that lawyers might have with this scientific approach to their issues. Using one of my own experiments for illustration, I try to convince my discipline that these concerns can at least be mitigated, if not completely dispelled, by the design of the experiment. I plead that the gain in knowledge, and in particular in reliability, outweighs the perceived cost of using a seemingly alien methodology.

The goal is of course not to turn all legal scholars into scientists. The prudential role of doctrinal law remains as important for society as ever, and the public will also not want to miss lawyers as public intellectuals. All I advocate is experiments as helpful complements to the legal discourse. One need not interpret legal rules as governance tools. But many lawyers do. If one does, it is important to know whether there is a governance problem in the first place, and whether legal intervention is able to improve the situation. In this reconstruction, social problems originate in human behaviour, and the law achieves its stated goals by impinging on human behaviour. Experiments help lawyers understand whether their reconstruction of the social problem is warranted, and whether the intervention is likely to deliver on its promises.

To make my point, I proceed in four steps. I illustrate the approach using one of my own experiments. I explain why the method has merit. I discuss the objections legal scholars might have. I finally go back to my experiment and demonstrate in which ways these concerns can be addressed.

2 An Illustration[1]

The German Copyright Statute stipulates:

> 'If the owner of a copyright has granted a licence such that the fee, in the light of the entire relationship between the parties, is grossly disproportionate with regard to the proceeds from the work, the buyer is obliged to agree, upon the author's request, to a change in the contract such that the seller receives an additional remuneration, reflecting what is her appropriate share under the given circumstances.' (§ 32a UrhG)

This is a regulatory invention. On first reading, the provision may seem odd. Why do the parties not write a success contingent contract? And why is the provision asymmetric? The copyright owner may ask for more money if the product flies. By contrast, the publisher may not ask her money back if the product flops. Seemingly the provision is nothing but another instance of the legislator subduing to pressure from an interest group. Since in Germany copyright owners are organized in powerful collection societies, this explanation would not be implausible.

My co-author and I wondered whether there is not more to this provision. The starting point of our analysis was a well-known fact from media economics. In this industry, success and failure are very unevenly distributed, and they are very difficult to predict, as illustrated by movie data (Figure 1).

1 This section uses material from C. Engel & M. Kurschilgen, 'Fairness Ex Ante and Ex Post. Experimentally Testing Ex Post Judicial Intervention into Blockbuster Deals', 8 *J Empirical Legal Studies*, 2011, pp. 682-708. For more detail, and statistical tests, see that publication.

Figure 1 Distribution of Earnings

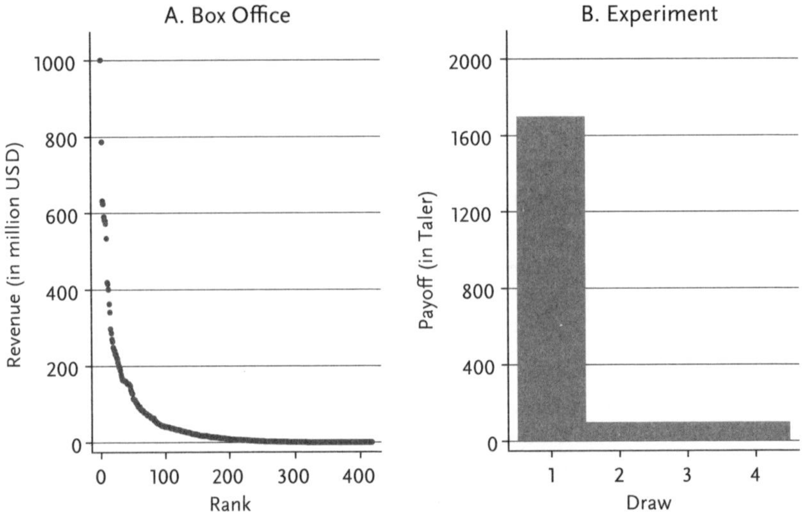

Note: Panel A depicts the worldwide gross box office revenues of the 450 most successful movies in 2008, according to boxofficemojo.com. Panel B illustrates the distribution of earnings in the experiment: In 1 out of 4 cases the commodity is worth 1700 Taler, and in 3 out of 4 cases the commodity is worth 100 Taler.

We hypothesized that the asymmetry and the unpredictability would result in a gap between the fairness assessment *ex ante* and *ex post*. If both parties maximize income, all copyrights should trade. The price should be some split of the expected earnings from the project. Since effectively so many projects fail, this would mean that, in retrospect, for most projects buyers pay too much, while they pay much too little for the rare successful projects. *Ex ante*, buyers might be averse to insuring sellers. *Ex post*, sellers might feel they have given away a valuable commodity for a nickel. We therefore expected fairness sentiments to interfere with profit maximization. A considerable amount of rights might not trade in the first place. In the unlikely but possible event of big success, copyright owners might want to inflict harm on whom they now perceive as one greedy exploiter. In a world where fairness matters, the seemingly odd provision might actually improve efficiency in that it helps more rights to trade.

To test these expectations, we designed an experiment that is meant to capture the essence of the potential fairness problem. We exposed randomly matched buyers (B) and sellers (S) to a payoff structure that closely matches the payoff structure in the movie market (Figure 1, Panel B). Three quarters of all projects only yield a small return, while one quarter is highly profitable. *Ex ante*, participants only know the distribution. We translate negotiations into the sequential game of Figure 2. At the outset, the buyer may make a take it or leave it offer. If the seller rejects, this round of the experiment is over. Both keep their identical initial endowments. There are no gains from trade. If the seller accepts, a random draw determines the profit from the project. This profit is received by the buyer. In the final stage, both players have the possibility to destroy income of the other player, at a small cost to themselves. This is our measure for hurt feelings of fairness *ex post*.

Figure 2 Baseline

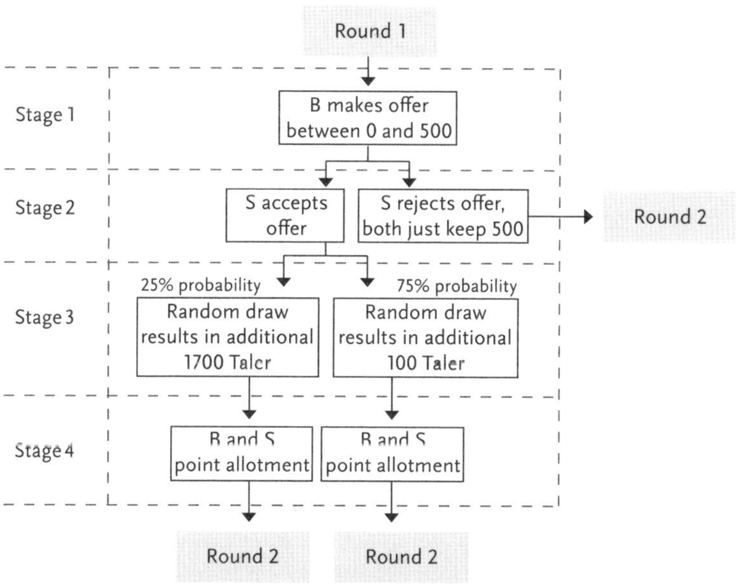

In the treatment, we add three more stages to the game. They are meant to capture the essence of the provision from German law. If the project is highly successful, a third player ('the umpire' U) freely determines the appropriate purchase price. This player receives a flat payment. The two parties know that this player has already taken a decision, but they do not know the amount. In the shadow of this unknown decision, they have an opportunity to renegotiate, using the same protocol as in stages 1 and 2.

Figure 3 Treatment

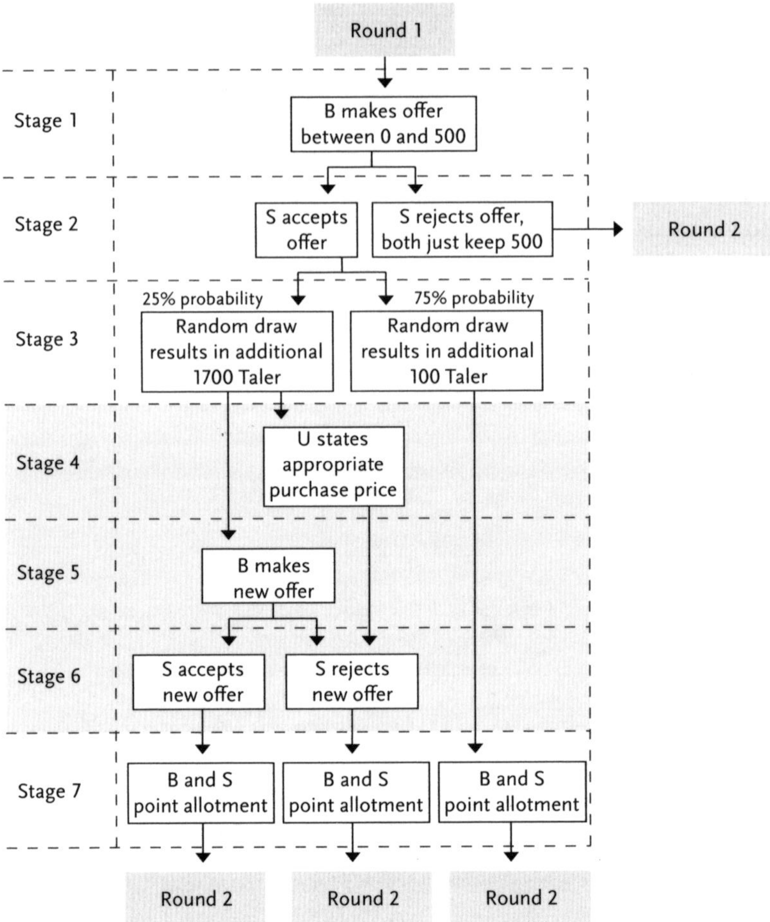

3 Promise

The hallmark of experiments is random assignment. There is a pool of independent events. In the case of economic experiments, these events are participants who are exposed to a well-defined environment. The experimenter draws a random sample from her much larger subject pool and, in the case of a single baseline and a single treatment, randomly assigns half of them to the former and half of them to the latter. If participants shall have different roles, as in our experiment, a further random draw defines whether they are sellers or buyers. If one wants to study how participants adapt to multiple, unknown interaction partners, re-matching is also by random assignment. Finally, provided the neutrally labelled commodity trades, the computer randomly decides, with the defined probability, whether the project has high or low value.

All these independent random draws make sure that statistically significant differences may be interpreted as support for the hypotheses. More technically even, the fact that the null hypothesis of no difference is rejected with sufficiently high probability shows that one has been unable to refute that null hypothesis. This careful language is warranted. In a strict sense, even the best experiment does not prove anything. The statement that the hypothesis is supported is conditioned on two things: the hypothesis and the design meant to test it are convincing; the unexplained variance in the data does not hide an overlooked explanatory variable. Even with the best possible empirical methodology, *i.e.*, with the randomized experiment, one never knows for sure. Yet if the experiment is carefully and adequately designed, and if the data analysis is flawless, this is the best possible evidence of a causal effect.

Defining and testing causes is essential both for legal interpretation and for legal policy making. For the interpreter, be it a court, a regulator, or the doctrinal scholar, understanding what the rule is meant to achieve is not the only possible, but a critical element in getting its interpretation right. Continental scholars would speak of teleological interpretation. For the legislator, a regulatory agency, or the legal scholar advising either of them, it is even more important to understand the purported social problem, and to forecast the effect of a proposed intervention.

In economics, the possibility to solve the identification problem by randomization is the main reason why scientists turn to experiments. With field data, true identification is often very difficult, if not impossible. Scientists are at the mercy of natural experiments. Naturally occurring random events are hardly ever as clean as the lab. And one may only study what, by some natural accident, was exposed to a random shock. For legal scholars, a second benefit from running experiments is equally important. Experiments make it possible to study phenomena that are hard, if not impossible to observe in the field. Happily, more and more law-related data sets are made available; this fuels the empirical legal movement. Yet many facts a doctrinal lawyer, or a legal policymaker for that matter, would ideally want to know do never enter such datasets. This in particular holds for counterfactuals. How would the law's subjects have reacted, had the existing rule been replaced by an alternative intervention?

Both advantages of the experimental method also materialize for our example experiment. Germany seems to be the only country to have a 'bestseller paragraph'. Aggregate data about the profitability of the media across national economies is available. Yet this would obviously not be sufficient for identification. There are many alternative, plausible explanations for a difference in earnings across countries. The German rule has been introduced at a defined moment. One might compare earnings before and after that moment. This would be better, but far from ideal. As usual, there had been a lengthy debate over the new rule. Any difference in earnings one might find might also result from strategic adjustments of interested actors to the prospect of rule change.

The possibility to observe the unobservable is even more valuable in our case. Contract patterns are not easy to observe. Neither copyright owners nor media enterprises have reason to make them public. Outside the lab, it is close to impossible to study the decision not to trade a copyright, in expectation of or after the failure of negotiations. If our hypothesis holds true, we should see that the assessment of which outcome is considered fair changes with the dissolution of the uncertainty. This requires observing fairness judgements before and after the random draw that decides on the profitability of the project. With the help of the experiment, we are also able to study the underlying process. We not only see whether, if the rule is in place, more deals are struck. We may also say something about the prices buyers offer, and we get a continuous measure of the degree by which sellers and buyers are dissatisfied with the final distribution of profits, conditional on the profitability of the project. We may even study how neutral authorities interpret the rule under standardized conditions.

4 Concerns

Many legal scholars are sceptical about the experimental method. Often these concerns are rather diffuse. Yet if the experimental approach to law is to make it, experimentalists are well advised to take concerns seriously. As good scientists, they should themselves be their most informed critics, and should start a discourse that assesses the validity of the concerns, and that discusses potential solutions. This lecture is meant as a contribution to this nascent discourse.

The concerns may be grouped into five categories: experiments might be seen as being too scientific, too individualistic, too narrow, too anxious, and too small. Let me address them each in turn.

4.1 Too Scientific

To my reading, the most prominent concern is the most obvious: experiments are a scientific technique. In many respects, this scientific approach seems alien to law. It appears too rigorous, too simple, too impractical, and too distanced.

Scientists have a taste for rigor. This is not only a culturally contingent trait. In a way, for science rigor is definitional. The epistemic goal of a scientist is objectivity. To assess the relevance and the quality of a scientific argument, the person of the scientist is immaterial. Scientists are interested in the argument per se. If someone completely unknown, or completely irresponsible for that matter, had made that same argument, it would count the same. If the argument has scientific value, it holds, irrespective of cultural context. The ideal objective language is mathematics.

To live up to this ideal of objectivity, all scientific work starts with the definition of a precise research question. If the scientist works empirically, she first translates this research question into an explicit hypothesis. Ideally, this hypothesis is derived from exact theory. In experimental economics, often even this theory is formal. In the process of defining the hypothesis, the scientist explicitly or implicitly excludes aspects of the real-life phenomenon that motivated her research question. In doing so, she makes assumptions. If she runs an experiment, these assumptions translate into the features of her design. Through narrowing down the field of observation to a well-defined problem, the scientist prepares the ground for the application of exact empirical methodology.

Scientists attempt to falsify. They take it for granted that no theory, and no empirical method, will ever completely address reality. Eventually, reality is too complex, and too little orderly, to be studied in an objective way. Scientists do not want to understand; they want to explain and, maybe, predict. Their goal is the production of generic knowledge. Through studying some instances of reality, they want to uncover the forces that lead to apparent homogeneity or heterogeneity. In so doing, they are proactively modest. They never claim they know. All they say is that, given the evidence they had been able to observe or, in a lab experiment, to generate, a theoretical expectation could not be falsified. If the evidence is probabilistic, as it usually is with experiments, they also quantify the trust one may have in this statement. This is the purpose of the ominous p-value, which is often represented by a number of stars.

In all respects, the traditional definition of legal scholarship differs. The epistemic goal is not objectivity but truth. Lawyers deliberately trade inter-subjectivity for the possibility of getting it right in the case at hand. Ultimately, lawyers are not observers, but actors. In legal practice, decisions are taken. Legal academics help those who take these decisions to make better decisions. The regulative ideal of law is the decision taken in an individual case. This decision must do the parties justice. Generic knowledge is welcome if it improves this decision. But ultimately, scientific knowledge is only one potential input. If a fact, or a purported causal relationship, cannot be proven to the requisite scientific standard, this does not automatically exclude them from legal argument. Features of the case may carry weight even if they defy scientific proof.

While scientists study problems they first have artificially constructed to be tractable, if they want to directly serve legal practice, legal scholars do not have this privilege. Real legal problems are always ill-defined, at least potentially. Even if the conflict of life that the rule is purportedly meant to address seems well understood, this never excludes the possibility that the next case reveals a hitherto overlooked, but normatively critical feature. A term from legal philosophy characterizes the difference between legal scholarship and science very well: the difference results from the open texture of all law. Legal rules are never completely defined. Potentially, any piece of legal wisdom may in every case of application be overruled. In a way, the fallibility of scientific knowledge makes it equally provisional. Yet in scientific argument, falsification is the ultimate purpose of the exercise. By contrast, in legal argument the tentative modification of a rule is a by-product of the attempt at striking a balance between predictability and justice.

The different epistemic goal translates into a different understanding of a result. A scientific result is a statement about conditional doubt. Given the design of the experiment, some theoretical expectations could be ruled out. For other explanations, in light of the evidence, the probability that a well-defined counter-statement holds true is very small. This is all scientists mean if they say they have a significant result. By contrast, the justification of a legal decision is presented as a fallible truth. Lawyers of course know that their decisions may be wrong. Yet if the decision has been taken by a competent authority, applying the pertinent procedural safeguards, the claim that the decision is wrong will only be heard in another formal procedure, for instance on appeal.

All science is partial analysis. Lawyers engage in total assessment. This is why they feel a scientific approach to law is too simple. Lawyers embrace the historical contingency of all observation. For them, a case is more than the manifestation of an abstract phenomenon, let alone a natural law. They are open to the un-orderliness of life, and they are happy to be surprised by a course of action or a driving force they have never seen before, and that has nowhere been documented. If there is no conceptual language for a phenomenon, this does not mean that this aspect of the case may be disregarded. If the phenomenon seems too complicated or too rich to be exactly defined, lawyers readily defer to their intuition.

Normative theorists grant that all normative argument starts from primitives that cannot be proven but must be agreed upon by a research community. In this sense, all normative argument is fundamentally relative. There is no uniform normative currency to trade higher welfare against more equitable distribution, higher perceived fairness, individual freedom or living up to the precepts of one's religion. If scientists argue normatively, they do so after having subscribed to one specific normative starting point. All of them can be shown to reflect different constructions of reality. By contrast, lawyers have to govern the lives of individuals who are neither under an obligation nor likely to adhere to a single normative perspective. In their decisions, lawyers have to navigate a multiplicity of conceptually unrelated normative expectations. In economic parlance, this gives the law a goal function with multiple arguments, all of which are allowed to be correlated with each other.

Economic theory is all about interested actors interacting with each other. Political science theory is all about the exercise of power. Scientists are certainly not blind to interested action, and to the resulting conflicts. Yet in the spirit of partial analysis, they tend to treat the investigation of individual or political conflict as a separate issue. Lawyers do not have that privilege. If a court gets a new case, the judge knows full well that the parties to the dispute are in conflict. Eventually, taming this conflict and restoring peace may even be more important than applying the law as it stands to the claim that has been brought. Yet in principle, judges are bound by the law. If the conflict is not unusually violent, they will try to remove the conflict precisely by finding out whether the claim is warranted in law.

Because the law wants to achieve so many things in parallel, the application of legal rules to facts is embedded into a rich institutional arrangement. The most important purpose of this procedural framework is to draw artificial boundaries. Once the court has decided, the losing party is only heard with the argument that the judgement is wrong in substance if she appeals the decision. If the time period for appeal has elapsed, the procedure may only be reopened under exceptional circumstances, for instance because new exculpatory evidence has become available. Likewise, once Parliament has passed a statute, the new rule assumes the force of law even if members of Parliament later concede that the decision was unwise. Even if it could be shown that the rule is anti-constitutional, this does not automatically invalidate it. It is for the Constitutional Court, pursuant another set of procedural rules, to decide upon constitutionality.

Law deliberately introduces additional degrees of freedom that give more room for manoeuvre, and to accommodate conflicting and incompatible expectations. Rule generation is separated from rule application. In the civil law countries, formally the courts do not have the right to make new law. In the common law countries, they do, but their law-making authority is tightly procedurally contained. While rule application, by the courts and administrative agencies, is different from openly adopting new rules, these authorities are able to gradually adjust the contents of the rule, in the light of the experience they are making in the current case.

A further possibility for addressing multiple audiences is the distinction between the generation and the representation of legal decisions. The motive for deciding the case in one way need not be the same as the explanation the judge gives to the party who has lost. The oral justification routinely differs from the written reasons. The former is meant to make the layperson understand the key reason. The latter are meant to demonstrate the legal community, and the appellate court in particular, how the decision fits into the established reading of the law.

Legal rules are governance tools. From a governance perspective, it matters whether a decision is perceived as appropriate. This conveys the individual decision, and the legal order more broadly speaking, output legitimacy. Yet perceived decision quality is only one source of legitimacy. Legitimacy also originates in the way how the applicable rule has come into being, and in the procedural safeguards attached to its application. For the time being, the governance effect is enhanced by predictability. The more reliably the law's subjects may forecast its effect, the better they will anticipate the regulatory constraint. They can adapt their behaviour and make explicit enforcement of the rule unnecessary. Yet there is a delicate balance between effective governance today and tomorrow. Each case potentially provides the legal order with an opportunity for learning. The technique by which the legal order strikes the balance between predictability and evolution is language. The courts are bound to the letter of the law. But they have to interpret these words. If new evidence or a better understanding of the conflict of life calls for it, they can adjust the meaning of the rule by cautious reinterpretation.

Lawyers must decide. This is why the discipline is, in a deep sense, pragmatic. Lawyers insist that a scientific approach may not deprive the law of its pragmatic viability. Lawyers are not allowed to defer the decision until sufficient scientific evidence has been generated. Lawyers are always under time pressure. Usually the acceptable duration of court procedure is not long enough for running a new experiment, even if that would make it possible to resolve a critical conflict over facts. Lawyers are rightly concerned that the assessment of the facts should not be too costly, neither for the parties nor for society. Eventually, lawyers are content with knowledge that is 'good enough', given the normative relevance of the case, the time available for deciding it, and the resources one may muster.

Finally, lawyers are sceptical about a scientific approach precisely because science aims at objectivity. In the scientific ideal, once a scientist has made a discovery, the discovery is completely distanced from the person of the scientist. The finding is not more relevant because it has been made by one specific scientist. For judging the quality of the finding, it suffices to check the reported method. By contrast, the law means to engage the decision maker as a person. Professional lawyers hold an office. They are permanently reminded that they decide on other people's lives. They are expected to take on responsibility for their decisions. The law does not want them to distance themselves from the outcome of the case. If the decision later turns out wrong it is their fault. The law means them to be aware of this when taking the decision.

4.2 Too Individualistic

If one adopts an experimental approach to law, one implicitly buys into an individualistic reconstruction of the social problem, and of the legal reaction. This program interprets law as an institution. Institutions are interpreted as purposeful interventions. They are reactions by the functional equivalent of a social planner to a perceived social problem.

For this intervention to be meaningful, the problem must originate in a difference between the actual individual action and the action that would be in everybody's best interest. The reconstruction program thus starts from a well-defined counterfactual. If the law remains inactive, a socially undesirable outcome is to be expected. Instead the law may also react to an observed state of affairs that violates an agreed-upon norm. The critical step is showing that this undesirable effect is caused by individual behaviour. In the standard rational choice framework, the social problem results from the interaction of perfectly informed, cognitively flawless, but selfish actors. The problem is exclusively motivational in nature. Individuals suffer either from a cooperation or from a coordination problem. In the former case, what is in everybody's best interest does not maximize individual profit. In the latter case, a game has multiple equilibria, and interested actors fail to coordinate on the socially desirable equilibrium, or on any equilibrium for that matter.

Behavioural theory and experimental evidence of course transcend this narrow definition of the social problem. They allow for much richer motivation functions, including socially more desirable motives, such as altruism, or socially even less desirable intentions, such as spite. They also model and test a host of cognitive limitations, like limited foresight, over-optimism, or loss aversion. Yet behavioural law and economics still reconstructs social problems as a divergence between actual and desired individual action.

Many lawyers feel that this creates an individualistic bias. Citizens are seen as isolated individuals, not as persons who take their identity from being members of a society, a nation, or a community. Consequently each individual citizen is seen as an isolated target for regulatory intervention. The opposing will, or the cognitive weakness, have to be overcome one by one. Lawyers are seen as social engineers. Based on superior knowledge, they correct individual mistakes.

Lawyers contrast this with an alternative reconstruction of the social problem. In this reconstruction, persons are social beings. They first and foremost lack orientation in a complex social environment which they know they at best partly understand. They look out for what is common in this environment. In this perspective, legal rules mainly serve an expressive function. They articulate social expectations. The main purpose of sanctions is not to overcome resistance, but to make it clear that society cares about these expectations, and that the social commitment to them becomes credible.

As a consequence, lawyers are also sceptical about the scope for institutional microsurgery. From the viewpoint of the individualistic program, the regulator need not have second thoughts when it tries to address one individual deviation from the optimum. By contrast, if individuals seek orientation, they are not unlikely to read as information about much broader social attitudes what was only meant as a cure for one specific problem. Interventions undertaken with the best of all intentions may prove counter-productive if they crowd out socially desirable behaviour in other areas of life. Such undesirable learning need not even be confined to the direct addressees of intervention, and may affect bystanders who merely observe how others are treated.

4.3 Too Narrow

A related concern starts from the observation that institutions are lumpy responses to lumpy (perceived) problems. By contrast, experiments are tools for identification and therefore tend to use miniscule manipulations to enable causal inference. There is a mismatch in the resolution, lawyers are afraid. In thought experiments, legal rules may well be decomposed into a combination of definable isolated effects. Yet in regulatory practice, interventions are never that clean. Actually, for the reasons laid out in the previous section, such micro-interventions may not even be desirable.

Moreover, in regulatory practice, institutions do not fall from heaven. They are also not imposed by a benevolent dictator. They result from institutional reform. Those advocating reform are hardly ever disinterested. Typically, they strive for distributional gain. At any rate, during the debate over reform the distributional implications are unlikely to be overlooked. Institutional reform is an act of policy-making. Lawyers are sceptical about advice that overlooks this political dimension.

In regulatory practice, there is no such thing as a perfect institution. Institutional reform at best gives an impulse. Whether this impulse brings society closer to the desired state of affairs depends on the reaction of addressees. Institutional addressees need not perceive a new intervention as guidance. They may instead try to combat what they perceive as a loss in opportunities, by creative attempts at gaming the system. While creativity is by definition unpredictable, lawyers would try to anticipate particularly fierce resistance, and they would try to do more than just intervene. The better the necessity of the intervention is communicated, and the more the procedure for adopting it seemed fair, the more there is hope that the institution will actually reach its stated goal. Success and failure of institutional reform also hinge on the zeal and skill of those entrusted with implementing it. Or in the words of Douglas North: institutions are like vessels. They must be properly designed and adequately manned.

4.4 Too Anxious

The next set of lawyers' concerns is more virtual than real, for the simple reason that you must yourself be an experimentalist to know about them. I am talking about the dirty laundry of the discipline.

Experimentalists have a hammer, and therefore a tendency to treat everything as a nail. While their papers are of course written differently, they tend to select research questions such that they lend themselves to the experimental test.

Experimental law and economics is still very young, which is why the next concern has not yet materialized very much. But once the experimental literature grows, as it has for instance in experimental economics, or in theoretical law and economics for that matter, there is a high premium for sophistication. Scientists want to make it into the best journals. Happily this tends to require a good story. But pushing the technological frontier is certainly a promising strategy as well. This creates temptation to select topics not for their relevance for the interpretation or evolution of law, but for the possibility to showcase one's technical ingenuity.

A related concern is already visible. The experimental method goes hand in hand with a scientific culture. In science, interest is in progress, not in the best match with a real-life phenomenon. The best recipe to publish well is a counterintuitive result. Support for something most everybody thought to be true, but nobody was completely sure about, is much less highly regarded. It is even harder to publish non-results. One had a well-founded expectation, or the legal discourse had it, and a cleanly designed experiment is unable to find the effect. For the legal discourse, such non-results would often be even more important than a significant treatment effect. Yet since a non-result is not the same as positively showing that a relationship does not exist, in most experimental disciplines such results risk ending up in a file drawer.

Very mundane considerations also impinge on the direction of experimental research. Some research questions would require too many participants. Others would require a design that is too taxing on the subjects. The more active the internal review board, the more their concerns, or just their predilections, change the design. Experimentalists may take a different route if that generates data that is easier to analyze. They may shy away from research questions if they would be asked to develop a formal model and lack the expertise, or do not find a competent co-author. Most experimental research is path dependent. Experimentalists tend to prefer tried and tested designs, to which they just add one manipulation. This protects them against unwanted surprises. It also helps them to address critics in a way that would be close to impossible with a standalone experiment.

Last but not least: peer review makes opportunistic. If the editor of a good journal has invited to resubmit a paper, next everybody literally follows her advice, even if they are not convinced that it is sound. In anticipation, many experimental papers are written defensively. Much energy is spent on pre-empting referee critique. Playing the peer review game well may eventually become more important than making a valuable contribution to the legal discourse.

4.5 Too Small

Finally, when they read experimental papers, lawyers in the doctrinal camp often wonder why so much energy is spent on so little. Not so rarely, they couch this reaction into the phrase: this my grandmother would have told you. The proverbial grandmother possesses the wisdom of life. She usually will not have explicit theory, let alone the ability to place a new result into a wider conceptual framework. But over a long, attentive life she may indeed have seen so much that she senses the result with her intuition. Intuition is a powerful generator of hypotheses. Since intuition is able to handle so much information, and to work even with inputs that are only tentative, intuition is an important ingredient in legal decision-making. Yet even if the result of the experiment is not counterintuitive, it may still be very valuable for the law whether an effect one thought might exist can actually be shown to exist. Not so rarely, it also improves legal decision-making if one knows the size of the effect. Intuition is much better at generating qualitative than quantitative assessment.

A related reaction of doctrinal lawyers is even more frequent: the law knew it all along. Actually this is quite often true. This is one of the reasons why the interaction between experimentalists and doctrinal lawyers is so productive. Doctrine is an almost never-ending source of powerful research questions that can be put to the experimental test. Law knows so much because the institutional arrangement is specialized on creating responsible decisions if all participating know that they do not know (enough). Rule generation and rule application are techniques for navigating an only partly understood environment.

Actually law not only locally tries to make the best out of the available imperfect information and understanding. Law is a very elegant, and a very powerful technique for permanently revising and improving rules. Since legal rules react to perceived social problems, legal evolution automatically also checks and improves the understanding of the underlying problem, and of the ability of different legal interventions to address it. While doctrine therefore is a precious container of social knowledge, the gems are usually uncut and unpolished. Quite often the law indeed knew before the experiment. Yet it only knew in a rather vague sense. Experiments help make this knowledge explicit. They sort between conflicting apparent pieces of legal wisdom. And they check to which degree what has been found in one area of law generalizes to other areas of law.

5 Solutions

I am not purporting to have a solution for all these concerns. I am also not trying to convey the idea that a one-size-fits-all solution is likely to be found. We will quite likely have to live with some tension between science and doctrine, between individualistic and social constructions of legal problems, between the conditions for causal inference and lumpy institutional choice, between the responsibility for legal development and the competitive pressure of peer-review, between intuition and explication. Yet in this final section, I want to demonstrate, with the example experiment from the beginning of the lecture, that the design of legal experiments, the way how the resulting data is analyzed, and how the paper is written, is able to mitigate quite a few of these concerns.

Let me begin with the main findings from the experiment:[2]

- The provision led to lower prices (Figure 4, Panel A).
- Offers were more likely to be accepted if the buyer ran no risk of a real loss (Figure 4, Panel B); recall that gains from trade were at least 100 tokens.

Figure 4 Prices and Deals

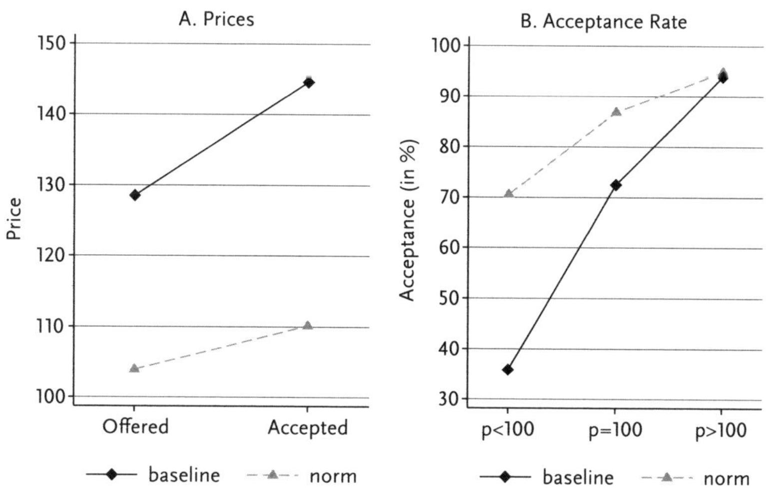

2 For statistical tests, please see the published paper.

- Authorities almost exclusively focused on *ex post* fairness (Figure 5) and ignored that the initial price had insured sellers against the risk of project failure.

Figure 5 Umpire Decisions

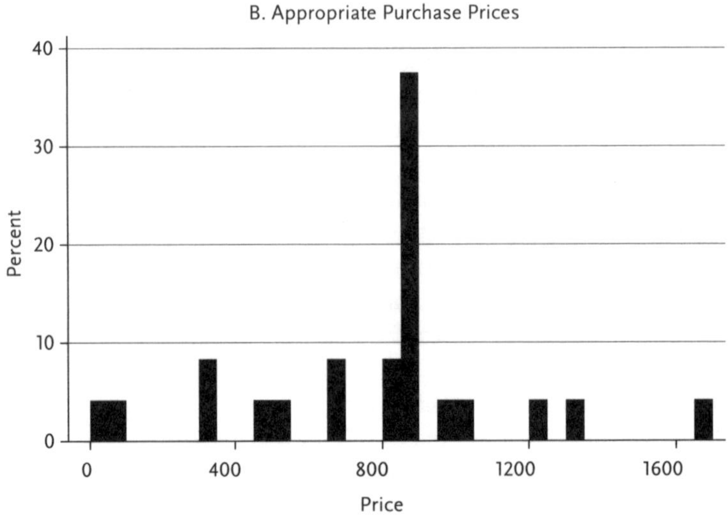

- Sellers hardly ever showed *ex post* discontent (Figure 6).
- Buyers showed more *ex post* discontent than sellers (Figure 6).
- Buyer discontent was reduced by the provision (Figure 6).

Figure 6 Punishment

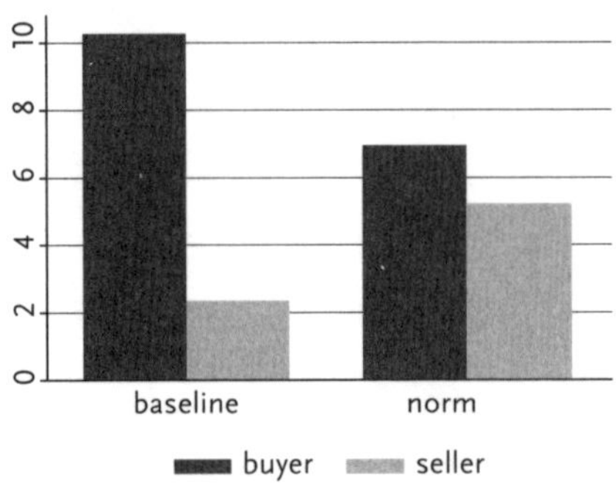

These clearly are scientific findings, with the characteristic limitations of scientific results. And yet doctrinal lawyers should have little reason to find them too scientific. It is for a German private law court to decide whether it interprets the provision from the copyright statute narrowly or broadly. This question would in particular come up if the court has to decide whether the license fee that had been paid before marketing the product in retrospect appears 'grossly disproportionate'. Likewise, it is for the legislators in other jurisdictions to decide whether they want to adopt the German rule. Were a publishing house to take the rule to the Constitutional Court, it would be for that court to decide whether the provision violates the constitutional protection of freedom of contract for no sufficiently important reason.

All these legal authorities, as well as their academic advisors, should find it relevant and useful to possess this new piece of generic knowledge. If the main purpose of regulatory intervention is assuaging hurt feelings of *ex post* fairness, the evidence is mixed. The umpire decisions demonstrate that there is indeed a strong sense that the buyer should not keep the entire profit if the product sells surprisingly well. Yet sellers seem to suffer much less from a violation of *ex post* fairness than one might have thought.

By contrast, in a narrow economic perspective, one might have expected a trade-off between efficiency and fairness. Seemingly the rule serves fairness at the price of weakening contract as a technology for decentralized coordination. Arguably, the court is an outsider to the media industry and therefore much less equipped to find the appropriate price than buyers and sellers. In anticipation of unpredictable or improper court intervention, buyers should be deterred from trading. One might expect that regulation creates a deadweight loss. The experiment not only shows that this plausible concern is ill founded. It even shows the opposite to be true. If success in the market is unpredictable, and if success contingent contracts are not practical, the party that risks being deterred is the publisher, not the copyright owner. In the absence of the possibility of *ex post* intervention, buyers must insure sellers by paying them a higher price ex ante. Otherwise they run the risk that all gains from cooperation get lost. If sellers know the legal order gives them renegotiation power in the unlikely event that the product is a big success, they accept lower prices. Buyers rightly anticipate this. The rule does not diminish, it increases efficiency.

This is of course only one input. Lawyers may well be dissatisfied that the rule does not seem to serve a real desire for *ex post* fairness. They may be concerned that authorities seem to neglect who has borne the entire marketing risk. They may still be suspicious that the promulgation of the rule is the result of lobbying, or the legislator believing that copyright owners have more votes than publishing houses. Or they may, to the contrary, believe that the rule is justified on distributional grounds, whether there is a fairness problem or not. In defining the 'appropriate' price, a court still needs detailed information about the concrete case.

Nonetheless, knowing that the provision enhances welfare should improve the quality of a decision in application of the rule. A judge who has a better understanding of the underlying conflict of life, and how it interacts with her intervention, stands a better chance to strike the right balance between the conflicting interests of the parties. Making this knowledge available does not put judicial responsibility at risk. To the contrary, it helps judges make a more responsible decision. The example experiment illustrates a beneficial division of labour. Precisely by using scientific methodology, experimenters can make knowledge available that matters for the decision of concrete cases, and for the adoption of new rules.

Some experiments aim at showing that standard economic theory gets it right even if many non-economists doubt it. A classic example is the double oral auction. In the lab and in the classroom it proves extraordinarily robust and almost surely leads to the market clearing price. Yet most experiments are designed because a researcher has the intuition, or increasingly exact theory, that makes her sceptical about the predictions of standard theory. The current experiment is part of the latter tradition. If sellers and buyers of copyright were risk neutral maximizers of profit with perfect cognitive abilities, the rule would be pointless. The distribution of gains from trade is common knowledge. Rational agents would not forego gains from trade, and they would price the opportunity adequately. Since our bargaining protocol gives the buyer all the bargaining power, she should offer the minimal increment above the sure gain, *i.e.*, 101 tokens, and the seller should accept with certainty. Of course, this is not what we see. Instead, with the help of the experiment, we learn how the conflict between *ex ante* fairness and bargaining power plays itself out and, critically, how the prospect of later neutral intervention changes these negotiations.

While we thus do not adopt a narrow definition of cognition and motivation, we indeed take an individualistic perspective. We do not study social practice in the media industry, or the social definition of identities on both sides of this market. We do not address whether the rule has changed what is seen as acceptable or desirable in this industry. Eventually, these questions would be easier to study with field data. But if one were to find an effect on the social construction of the conflict, one might want to know how this change has been brought about. One of our findings contributes to this. If the rule is in place, sellers are substantially and significantly more likely to accept offers below or at 100 tokens. With the rule, *ex post* buyer dissatisfaction is reduced. This suggests that the rule helps the parties transform a bargaining conflict into a trust relationship. Sellers are less likely to force buyers into incurring a real loss in the likely event that the project fails. Buyers can reciprocate by granting part of the profit in case the project is highly successful. Even if they do not, sellers have no reason for concern because, then, the authority assists them.

The experiment is unusual in that it puts a complete institution to the test. Between the baseline and the treatment, we change three things: we introduce a third party and give it power to change the price; we give the parties the opportunity to renegotiate if the project has been highly successful; through the rule we introduce an exogenous fairness focus. From the perspective of basic science, this is a problem. We are not able to say whether one of these features in isolation is causal for the effects we see. If these three causes interact, we do not know whether they are additive, substitutes or complements. We also cannot quantify the relative importance of either cause. This is the price we have to pay for our attempt to make a more direct contribution to the legal debate. We wanted to manipulate the presence of what we see as the core of the German rule.

Has our design being too strategic? In all honesty, it is not free from strategic elements. We originally had planned to derive hypotheses from a formal behavioural model. We have dropped the model since this would have forced us to quantify the threat of punishment in the same currency as gains from trade. While this would have captured the design of the experiment – punishment is in the same tokens as the proceeds from the project – this would not have resonated well with *ex post* discontent, which we want to capture by punishment.

But in many respects, we have not been anxious. We have not used a standard experimental design, but translated the essence of the provision into a new design. We have introduced an un-incentivized third player since judges are not paid by the benefit they do the winner. Note that, in experimental economics it is almost definitional that all choices must be incentivized to be credible. A further unusual feature of our design is punishment as a measure for hurt feelings of fairness. When we presented the experiment to an audience of experimental economists, one senior figure in the field accused us of 'giving participants a Molotov cocktail'.

Would my grandmother have told you? I cannot ask her any longer. She had a lot of common sense. But even with all admiration for my beloved grandmother, I doubt she would have predicted that sellers do not sense a fairness problem *ex post* while buyers do. She might have guessed that authorities will narrowly focus on the situation as it stands when they are called in. But I am sceptical she could have described in which ways the institution turns out efficient.

I do however want to stress that, indeed, the law knew it all along. The project has been worth doing precisely because one could plausibly think we had spotted an instance of failed legislation. The experiment proved necessary to uncover the hidden wisdom of what looked like an odd rule. This is not the only, but a promising route for experiments on legal issues. Lawyers should be wary that experiments are a challenging endeavour. But if they are done properly, legal experiments are not mission impossible, but a highly rewarding enterprise.

Ik heb gezegd.